TOM DALEY

Roy Apps

Illustrated by Chris King

First published in 2013 by
Franklin Watts
338 Euston Road
London NW1 3BH

Franklin Watts Australia
Level 17/207 Kent Street
Sydney NSW 2000

A CIP catalogue record for this book
is available from the British Library.

(ebook) ISBN: 978 1 4451 1838 3
(pb) ISBN: 978 1 4451 1834 5
(Library ebook) ISBN: 978 1 4451 2469 8

1 3 5 7 9 10 8 6 4 2

Printed in Great Britain

Franklin Watts is a division of Hachette Children's Books,
an Hachette UK company.
www.hachette.co.uk

Chapter One:

The Dream

"Oh, wow!" five-year-old William exclaimed to his older brother, Tom.

The Central Park Pool in Plymouth was packed with giant inflatables of every shape and colour. The pool was putting on a special kids' fun session.

While they were changing, William said: "I'm going to jump on the inflatables!"

"I'm going down the water slide," said Tom, who was seven.

As they ran out of the changing rooms, Tom suddenly stopped. Next to the main pool, there was a smaller one.

People were jumping off springboards into the water. Tom looked up. At the top of the tower, right up under the ceiling, stood a figure. He was perfectly still and looked very, very small. He stepped to the edge of the platform and Tom held his breath as the man dived in.

Tom stood there, amazed, watching the divers jumping into the water. His mum came up to him.

"Aren't you going on the inflatables, Tom?" she asked.

Tom shook his head.

"What about the water slide, then?"

Tom shook his head again.

"So what do you want to do?"

"That," declared Tom, pointing to the next diver preparing to jump off the 10-metre platform, the highest of them all.

Every Saturday morning Tom's mum and dad paid for him and his little brother William to have diving lessons. Each time Tom learned something new, he got a certificate which he hung in his room.

The following year, when Tom was eight, the 2002 Commonwealth Games were on TV. Tom watched all the diving events, amazed at the way the divers twisted and somersaulted through the air before splashing into the water. The British divers Leon Taylor and Pete Waterfield became Tom's heroes, together with the Canadian diver Alexandre Despatie, who had won a Commonwealth gold medal when he was just thirteen.

Tom's dad watched the Commonwealth Games with him. "If you think this is big," he said, "wait till they show the Olympic Games in a couple of years."

Tom looked puzzled. He had never heard of the Olympic Games.

"The Olympic Games," his dad explained, "is the biggest sporting event in the world. The next Olympics is in a couple of years in Athens. Then in Beijing in 2008. After that, well, they reckon that London is going to bid for the 2012 games."

Tom went upstairs to his room. He drew a picture. It was of a boy in a pair of Union Jack Speedos doing a handstand. Then Tom drew the Olympic rings and wrote "London 2012" on the paper. The picture was called "My Ambition".

Eight-year-old Tom Daley had a dream: to dive at the 2012 Olympic Games in London.

Chapter Two:

Measuring Up

Just before Tom's ninth birthday, he was invited to join the Central Park Pool's junior competitive diving squad. They were called "The Weenies". Tom's coach, Sam, was pleased with his progress.

"You are lucky, Tom," she told him. "You're one of the few people who are able to 'feel' where your arms and legs are when you're doing somersaults and twists. That means you've got a better chance of being able to do a really good dive."

Tom often stayed behind after lessons to do a bit more swimming and diving. One day, he was making his way back to the changing rooms after a couple of dives, when he suddenly felt dizzy. The other people at the side of the pool looked all blurry. Then he looked and saw a bright red puddle of blood in the pool. It was his blood! He'd hit his head on the side of the pool when he dived in.

Tom's mum rushed him to hospital, where the doctors stitched up the wound. The accident had taught Tom a very basic lesson about the sport of diving: it can be very dangerous.

In 2003, Tom's diving club in Plymouth hosted the National Novices event for young divers new to the sport. Tom picked up a silver medal. He was showing it off to his friends afterwards, when a woman approached him and

said, "My name's Chelsea Warr. Could you spare me a moment, Tom?" She asked Tom to do a couple of dives. Then she took out a tape measure.

"Arms out!" Chelsea instructed. Tom stretched out his arms and she measured them. Then she measured the length of his legs.

"That's great!" Chelsea told him at last. "Tom, I'd like to offer you a place on World Class Start. It's a programme for young divers funded by the National Lottery. We've got a weekend training camp coming up in September. We'd like you to join us."

"Yes!" thought Tom. "A whole weekend away without my mum and dad and my little brothers!"

Once he was away on the weekend though, he didn't feel quite the same. He enjoyed the diving and the training, but at bedtime he got really homesick.

His mum and dad came and picked him up. They bought him a toy monkey to cheer him up. The monkey became Tom's lucky mascot and travelled with him all over the world.

Soon, Tom was doing three training sessions a week in the practice harness at the Central Park Pool with his coach,

Sam. Tom was just ten when he was selected to go to his first international competition in Aachen, Germany. There, he won silver and bronze medals.

Tom continued entering competitions and going to the World Class Start training camps. Despite still getting homesick, his diving continued to improve. Between November 2003 and May 2005, Tom was unbeaten in his age group. He had also been identified by the Talented Athlete Sponsorship Scheme as a young athlete who could win a medal at the 2012 Olympic Games.

It seemed that nothing could stop Tom now.

two years earlier, Tom had won his first international medals. Everyone expected Tom to do even better this time.

Tom was diving from the 10 metre platform, the highest of the lot. His first dive was good. His second dive was even better. But as he climbed up the steps for his third dive, he suddenly froze. He couldn't put one foot in front of the other. His head was full of doubts. He was terrified he'd land flat

on the water again, as he had a couple of weeks earlier. An image flashed through his mind of hitting his head on the side of the pool when he was younger. He started shaking with fear.

Slowly, step by step, Tom climbed back down the ladder.

As he reached the poolside, he heard the announcement over the loudspeaker system. "Tom Daley. Third dive." By now there were tears in his eyes. He didn't stop walking until he reached the row where his mum and dad were sitting.

"What's wrong, Tom?" asked his mum.

Tom just shrugged.

"You sure you don't want to go back and have another try?" Tom's dad asked him, softly.

Tom shook his head, sadly. He felt so ashamed of himself. His mum and dad had come all the way from England to see him win a medal, and he'd let them down. He'd let everybody down. He didn't ever want to step onto a diving board again. He was sure that if he did, that same dreadful feeling of fear and panic would sweep over him once more.

Chapter Four:

Regaining Confidence

For nine whole months Tom didn't go up onto the 10 metre diving platform. "What's wrong with you, Tom?" asked the other divers. Tom didn't know. The only thing he was sure of was that his career as a diver was over.

One day Tom said to his coach, "What's wrong with me?"

"I'm not sure," his coach replied. "But I have heard of the sort of thing you're going through happening to other athletes, especially in those sports where you have to launch yourself into the air, like diving, trampolining and gymnastics. Do you know any gymnasts?"

"I'm friends with Beth Tweddle on Facebook," said Tom.

"Why not have a word with her?" suggested Tom's coach.

Beth Tweddle, World and European Champion gymnast, told Tom that she'd had similar feelings of fear herself at one time, but that she had managed to get over them. "It's a psychological thing," she explained.

The British Diving Sports Psychologist, Michelle Miller, explained to Tom that his fear of diving was called Lost Movement Syndrome. "Obviously, leaping off a 10 metre platform is dangerous," she told Tom. "What happens is that your brain starts sending out warning signals to your body, to tell it not to do something that could risk harming you."

So Tom worked hard with his coach to improve his mental preparation for diving. Eventually, he regained his confidence and was able to face the 10 metre platform again.

Once he'd managed to do that, the training started to go well — very well. In January 2007, despite being three years younger than the usual minimum age, Tom was allowed to compete in the Australian Youth Olympic Festival. Later that same year, he won the senior platform title at the English Amateur Swimming Association National Championships. He began to compete on the international diving circuit and achieved two fourth place finishes. At the end of the year he qualified for the Beijing 2008 Olympics.

Tom didn't win a medal at the Beijing Olympics, but he relished the experience. After the Olympics, he enjoyed taking part in the parade around London with the other members of Team GB. Thousands of people lined the streets waving Union Jacks and foam hands and taking pictures. "Wow," Tom thought, "if this is what happens at a post-Olympic tour, what is the atmosphere at the London 2012 Olympics going to be like?"

Tom knew he was well on track for achieving his dream of diving at the London 2012 Olympics. He was young, he was strong and he'd overcome his fear of the 10 metre platform.

But something was about to happen that would shatter Tom's world forever.

Chapter Five:
Losing Dad

Tom's diving continued to go well. He became the youngest ever European Champion when he won the 10 metre platform title. In 2009, he became the 10 metre platform world champion.

At each of these events, Tom was accompanied by his greatest supporter, his dad, Rob.

Rob had been ill with a brain tumour a few years earlier, but it was thought he had made a full recovery. Then one day, he woke up with a terrible headache. At the hospital, the doctors found that he had another tumour at the back of his head. Three days later, he lost all movement in his left side.

For Tom, it was terrifying. Although Rob was still trying to keep cheerful and jokey, Tom knew that his dad was seriously ill. As the eldest, Tom had to try to act normal for his little brothers, William and Ben.

When Tom went to India for the 2010 Commonwealth Games, it was the first competition he had been in where his dad wasn't there to cheer him on.

In the final of the individual 10 metre platform event, he needed to dive well to beat the reigning Olympic Champion, Matt Mitcham, from Australia.

Tom's first two dives were good, but would they be good enough? His last dive was an inward three-and-a-half somersaults with tuck — something he had struggled with in the past. As he surfaced after the dive, he knew it had gone well, but he didn't realise just how well. The judges all awarded him straight 10s — the perfect score! Tom was Commonwealth 10 metre platform champion. The first thing he did was phone home to let his dad know.

Tom's dad was well enough to see him at the World Series competition in Sheffield in April 2011. There he won

gold in the 10 metre synchronised platform with Peter Waterfield, whose diving had inspired Tom back in 2002.

Straight after that, Tom flew off to Mexico for another international competition. He was about to fly out to a training camp in the US, when his mum rang.

"Tom, you've got to come home," she told him. Tom knew it was serious. "There's a flight booked. You've got to be at the airport in an hour's time. Your dad hasn't got long to live."

Tom couldn't believe what was happening. Although he'd known that his dad's illness was life threatening, somehow — deep down — he'd convinced himself that one day his dad would get better.

When he got home the next day, Tom found that his family had made up a special bed for Rob in the front room. Tom carried on going to training, but found it impossible to concentrate.

On 27 May 2011, Tom's dad died.

Chapter Six:

London 2012

Three months after his dad's funeral, Tom went to London, where special celebrations were marking the fact that it was "one year to go" until the 2012 Olympics. Tom was given the honour of

making the first ever dive at the new
Aquatics Centre.

Tom missed his dad, but he continued
with his training and competing,
preparing himself for the Olympics. He
knew his dad would have wanted him
to carry on.

Three months before the Olympics, he
regained his European 10 metre

platform title. In the British Championships the following month, he took the 10 metre individual title.

But he knew that at his home Olympics, the eyes of the world would be on him as never before. His first event was the 10 metre synchronised platform with Peter Waterfield.

But Pete and Tom's event did not go well. They missed out on a medal, finishing in fourth place. To many people, it seemed as if Tom's confidence had deserted him. Things got worse when in the preliminary round for the 10 metre platform individual event, Tom turned in a poor performance, finishing 15th out of the 18 divers who qualified for the next round.

But one fan continued to text Tom with messages of support. That fan was

David Beckham. "Keep your chin up!" he wrote. "It's not that bad."

It wasn't long before Tom was climbing the ladder for his first dive of the 10 metre platform individual finals. As he dived, camera flashes in the crowd dazzled him. He was distracted and disorientated. Tom managed a score of only 75 points, nowhere near enough to put him in the hunt for a medal.

Both Tom and his coach lodged a complaint with the referee, and Tom was allowed to take his dive again. This time he scored 91.80.

As he stepped onto the platform for his final dive, Tom knew that if he could give it everything and produce the dive of his life, he was in with a chance of a medal. Far below him, 17,500 people strained their necks to see him. His

mum was down there with his brothers and grandparents. He thought of his dad and knew he had to do this dive for him.

Tom breathed deeply, calmed himself and then leapt out off the board and into the unknown.

He felt the familiar sense of freedom and weightlessness as he spun through the air. He completed four-and-a-half brilliantly executed somersaults before he splashed into the water.

As he came to the surface, Tom looked up and saw that his scores were good — very good. The Aquatics Centre filled with thunderous cheering.

Tom had won a bronze medal. He had become the first British individual diver in 52 years to win an Olympic medal.

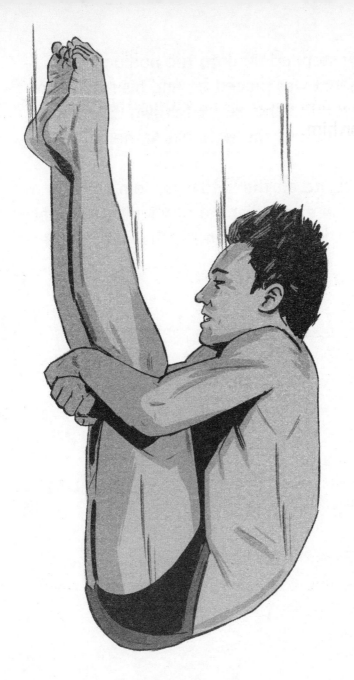

He stepped up onto the podium. The medal was placed around his neck. Tom waved to the excited crowd. Everyone roared out the National Anthem.

Despite all the setbacks, Tom's dream as an eight year old of winning a medal at the London Olympics had come true.

Fact file
Tom Daley

Full name: Thomas Robert Daley

Born: 21 May 1994, Plymouth, England

Height: 1.77 metres

Major Medals

- **2008 Junior World Championship (Aachen)**
  Silver, 10 metre platform
  Silver, 3 metre springboard

- **2008 European Championships (Eindhoven)**
  Gold, 10 metre platform

- **2009 World Championships (Rome)**
  Gold, 10 metre platform

- **2010 Commonwealth Games (Delhi)**
  Gold, 10 metre platform
  Gold, synchronised platform (with Max Brick)

- **2012 Junior World Championships (Adelaide)**
  Gold, 10 metre platform
  Gold, 3 metre synchronised springboard (with Jack Laugher)

- **2012 European Championships (Eindhoven)**
  Gold, 10 metre platform

- **2012 Olympic Games (London)**
  Bronze, 10 metre platform

Other Honours

2007, 2009, 2010 BBC Young Sports Personality of the Year (the only person to have won this award more than once)

Catch up with all the latest news about Tom at: www.tomdaley.tv

Rebecca Adlington

The 14-year-old girl stood on the side of the pool in the final of the 2003 European Youth Olympics 800 metres freestyle. As the swimmers dived in, the arena echoed noisily with shouts and cheers from the spectators. "Come on, Becks!" shouted the girl's family from their seats in the crowd. The girl touched the finishing wall in second place. Afterwards, her family and friends crowded around to congratulate her for winning the silver medal. A man approached the girl's mum. "That was a brilliant race your daughter swam," he said. "I think she's got potential. My name's Bill Furniss, by the way. I'm a professional swimming coach and I'd like to offer to coach your daughter."

Continue reading this story in:
DREAM TO WIN:
Rebecca Adlington